Why she flew to Barcelona

Eddie Gibbons

CALDER WOOD PRESS

2010

Why she flew to Barcelona, by Eddie Gibbons

Published by **Calder Wood Press**
1 Beachmont Court, Dunbar, EH42 1YF
www.calderwoodpress.co.uk

ISBN: 978-1-902629-31-5

Copyright © Eddie Gibbons 2010

All rights reserved. No part of this publication may be reproduced or transmitted in any form or by any means, electronic or mechanical, including photocopy, recording or information storage and retrieval system without permission in writing from the publisher.

The right of Eddie Gibbons to be identified as author of this work has been asserted in accordance with Section 77 of the Copyright, Designs and Patents Act, 1988

Cover design by Eddie Gibbons

Acknowledgments: *The First Time I Met Algebra* is also published in the anthology *At Grand Central Station We Sat Down and Wept* (Red Squirrel Press, 2010). *Aussie Mandias* has connections with P B Shelley's *Ozymandias*.

Printed by LEVENMOUTH PRINTERS, Muiredge, Buckhaven, Fife, KY8 1JH www.levenmouthprinters.co.uk The papers are derived from wood pulp originated from forests managed for long-term sustainability.

I'M MORE TH>N	5
LOVE IN THE TIME OF CORELDRAW	6
REMEMBERING MOROCCO	7
TWILIGHT TALONS	8
AMSTERDRAM	9
THE ANECDOTE OF THE DOOR	10
AUSSIE MANDIAS	11
OBAMARAMA	12
RIPCORD	14
SUTRA	15
THE FIRST TIME I MET ALGEBRA	16
CRASHING ACROBATS	17
TÊTE À TATE	18
MODERNIST LOVE	18
ROTHKO FOR DUMMIES	19
RESOLUTION	19
VINNOCENCE	20
ANOTHER OLD PHOTOGRAPH POEM	20
VENUS INFERS	21
DA CAPO	21
HANNIBAL LECTERN	21
NOT ANOTHER BILLY COLLINS POEM	22
STEREOTYPE	23
JOHN MOTSON MEETS EMILY DICKINSON	24
THE PARADOX OF THE TWINS	26
IN VIGIL, LATER	28
RUNNING OUT OF WORLD	29
THE ONLY WAY OUT	29
HARD TO SWALLOW	30
IF YOU SEE A MAN	31
AT THE TOMB OF THE UNKNOWN ACCOUNTANT	32
A TERRACEFUL OF MARILYNS	34
WHY SHE FLEW TO BARCELONA	35
VOICE BOXING	36

I'M MORE TH>N

More Lada than Prada
More NYPL than DKNY
More Vague than Vogue
More Ball Boy than Balmain
More Lager Lout than Lagerfeld
More Mascherano than Moschino
More Villanelle than Coco Chanel
More Vest Vest Vest than Est Est Est
More Harvey Smith than Harvey Nicks
More Charity Store than Christian Dior
More Kev and Tosh than Becks and Posh

More Stella Artois than Stella McCartney
More Anna Karenina than Donna Karan
More Aphra Behn than Oprah Winfrey.
More Red Adair than Fred Astaire
More Eastwood than Westwood
More Berryman than Burberry
More Belafonte than Beyonce
More Syllable than Sellable
More Pub than Published
More Owing than Ode

LOVE IN THE TIME OF CORELDRAW

Once I would have laid a rosebud at your feet,
sent a scented missive in an envelope delivered
by a go-between; stood beneath your window
in a blizzard of snowdrops, hoping for a glimpse
of your shadow in the moonlight.

But times have altered the language of the heart.
The lexicon of longing is no longer written longhand,
with soaring serifs scribed in ink on beds of vellum,
but by illuminated texts on Ericssons and Vodafones,
and new-millennium lovers go Blackberry picking down
lanes of pay-and-go, past Oranges and Apple phones.

Once keystrokes onto paper kept the rhythm of romance:
ribbons bled red streams of yearning, or keys rapped
out the stuttering sentiments of nervous suitors onto
scented sheets of lavender, which they sent, post-haste
to beloveds in lanes and streets and avenues.

These days my words to you are more mobile
and predictable: more to the pointer, more pithy,
more reducible, and so, my love, I offer you these tokens
on my part- my dingbats, my emoticons, my clip-art heart.

REMEMBERING MOROCCO

Walking into the Barber's shop I clock
the mirrored features of a colleague
I worked with twenty years ago.

He's busy having his head arranged
by the hairdresser, like a mannequin
being coached for a shop window display.

It isn't until he's walking out that he
recognizes me. I say we seem only to
meet once every World Cup.

*Remember last time – that bar in Lyon,
en-route to St. Etienne?*

Me, the lone Englishman
suddenly surrounded by a troop of tartans,
when his voice broke from the ranks,
a bugle call from the 5th Cavalry cresting
the ridge, to rescue me from my alien accent.

And just how dire was that Morocco game?

He corrects me, saying no, that wasn't the
last World Cup. What about Japan and Korea?

My God! Was that match really eight years ago?

We swap current addresses and he exits,
having shorn me of four years worth
of memories, which have fallen from me
and gather grey, lifeless, cropped, around
my feet.

TWILIGHT TALONS

I swim in luminescence in my insulated room.

A book glows on my lap. The TV beams
its satellite streams back towards the moon.

Its reflection flickers on my windowpane.

My glowworm world is protected by a thin
skin of science: the membrane of modern
magic repels the alchemy and spells of that
dark terrain beyond the pane.

The night is an enormous cave where
horn and tooth and claw conspire
to reap their crimson harvest.

Out there
bats scrape the night with sonar; owls scoop
blood by beakfuls, hawks rake their shrill reports
across the moonless moors.

The sounds claw at the pane.

Darkness has wings, and the twilight talons,
out there where feather wreaks its vengeance
on fur.

A small point of life drinks my light; a moth
wafts its way towards my reservoir of brightness,
to be impaled by a scything starling.

Only its thin pain between us

AMSTERDRAM

It's Amsterdam - it's Amstel, ham
with mustard, it is ice cold beer.
The company pass muster- a gentleman
from Munster with his nice old dear.

It's summertime, rosy wine; swallows
rising up and circling the square.
Cavalcades of bicycles rattle down
the cobblestones, shaking up the riders'
bones, hurtling in a blur.

Down the Zuider Zee side,
figures at the quayside
where canal boats cruise,
were canal boats' crews.

Fitters on the leeside work canal boat screws.

Red Light District misses in tight restricted dresses
ask for lights from misters in the Fondlepark dark.
Two lips red as tulips will whisper to each punter:

The wisdom down from Haarlem-
from the Charter of the Harlot –

It's dismal in the charnel,
get your carnal while you can.

Scoff a Space Cake, down a jug,
clack your clogs on Magere Brug.
See Vermeerkat and Rem Brand.
Sink another Amsterdram.

THE ANECDOTE OF THE DOOR

When I arrived
the door was bolted,
the windows shuttered.

Inside,
there was super-
heated conversation:

whys, wherefores;
a blamestorming
session,

but
she answered a question
I had not uttered-

when I departed
I noticed the door
had been left open

to anyone.

AUSSIE MANDIAS

I met a traveller from Down Underland
Who said: *Two fat and vestless Poms from Cromer
Drove through the desert*. Rusting in the sand,
Half sunk, a knackered Vee Dub lies, whose owner's
Crinkled lips craved beer from colder hands,
Such as a barmaid's, who well his passion read,
I Will Survive stamped on her underthings:
The hands that rocked him and the heart that bled.
And in her diary these words appear:
*His name was Aussie Mandias, King of Things
That Work, Are Mighty, But Need Repair!*
Nothing bedside remains. Call the AA?
Round that Vee Dub's decay, beyond her care,
Forlorn and endless sands scorch through the day.

(With apologies to P.B. Shelley)

OBAMARAMA

When America opened Ellis Island for its immig-
ration ration, it didn't offer to bring those *muddled
asses* true ad-liberty, e-quality and fat-earn-ity,
but they got it. *You got it!* Then this supersized superpower
was usurped in the hour between the first and second tower.

A woman sat on the bus from Montgomery, Alabama,
December 1955. An Americafrican by dissent, Rosa parked
herself in a seat meant only for Whites. She was Kilimanjaro
disguised as a seamstress. She budged not an inch.
She stitched up the Klan and started a boycott. Sparked
a riot of rage at her bus stop, where the black buck stopped.

When America's 1960 U2 *Black Lady* tour bombed
after playing tick with MiGs and I-Spy with ICBMs,
the KGB made a POW of Powers and the old Cold War
escalated faster than the rush in Krushchev.

When the me in America met the us in Russia,
offshore Cuba, '62, trigger fingers hovered over
the but in button but deployment of Misguided Missiles
was averted by calming the egos of nations in negotiations.

Because the i in America accepted the lone shooter posit
in Depository, shunning Zapruder and sassy Knoll theorists,
the sin in assassin stayed singular when Oswald swallowed
the Ruby bullet and a small child saluted a riderless horse.

Viet Cong spooks dug foxholes in Nixon's subconscious.
Conscientious students were shot in Clark Kent State, Ohio,
as William Calley, *Lieutenant Shithead*'s collateral thinking
caused all the damage and damaged the cause, while those
who survived both Tet and Long Tan tell *My Lais* about Vietnam.

The art of Martin Luther's rhetoric resided in the lack in black,
the kin in King and the mend in amendment. Whereas a white
Englishman warned of rivers of blood, an American negro spoke
only of rivers. He dreamed the dream. The dream came true
and altered the hue of the American panorama.

O, Rosa! O, Langston! O, Bama!

RIPCORD

It's the red-eyed Early Bird again today,
the pre-dawn flight, ABZ to MCR.
Drawn to your ward on the wings
of a jet; its engines throttling,
lifting and descending but leaving
me hovering at 20,000 feet,
surrounded by the endless stars
in their countless constellations,
backlit by the thin arc of sunrise
bathing the rim of the planet
in primordial light, suspending me
in this purgatory: the thought of you
dying expanding through my universe
like a parachute opening
inside my lungs.

SUTRA

I've never had casual sex.
No – it's always been frantic –
in the pantry, in the kitchen,
up in the attic.

But frankly, those antics had to stop
when I reached 60. Nothing nifty
or athletically nimble fitted the bill.

The new drill involved a bucket
of pills, creams, an ocean of lotion
just to get a semblance of motion.

Then I discovered the art of Tantra.
That long-sought-after *calmer* sutra.

Two weeks to prepare for a kiss?
Bliss.

THE FIRST TIME I MET ALGEBRA

my first line of defence was to attack it
with anagrams; but *grab ale*, *a garble*, even
bare gal were not enough to cure the trauma.

My former fear was long division-
those Babel-towering numerals spoke
no language that I knew: I was number dumb.

My mathematics were derisory, my thematic
was prosody. No rosy future beckoned me
from the thorny bush of numeracy.

Algorithms gave me the blues.
Quadratics ruled the roots in schools.
Fractions made me fractious.

I was top of the form in despondency
until a classmate reminded me that
x and y are the last two letters of *sexy*.

So I wrote a sexy poem for her
about how an x wanted to get a y
between satin sheets of parentheses

but I received the same rejection as
my maths exam submission –
were you born stupid, or do you practise?

On my way home from school I noticed
a woman weeping by the railway station.
No need to guess. I knew: my maths teacher.

CRASHING ACROBATS

Being the on-call I.T. man, Henry
had been summoned by the Help Desk
and told to fix the problem on Jane's computer-
her Acrobat kept crashing.

A female name always perked him up.
In seconds flattered, Henry was dashing,
not in a Mills & Boon way,
but heading Jane's way to fix her PC.

It was love at first smite when she
saw him in the sheen of her screen.
He's more Ryanair than debonair,
she thought, *but he'll do for me.*

*I hope she's more Easy Jet
than Virgin,* he thought back.

Henry wanted his hardware
inside her software so much
that he silently saluted her
from the depths of his Calvins.

Jane caught his glance the way
a trapeze artist catches her partner's
outstretched talcumed hands.

Neither of them noticed the absence
of a safety net.

TÊTE À TATE

This earnest lad with his Debenhams Diva
imagines himself a bristling bridegroom,
little knowing this relationship will stretch him
like a canvas to the limit, unaware
how much he'll fracture, or how quickly
love's lava cools from lover to hater, from
love her to *hate her*, from glider to Stuka –
how the lily fields turn into battlefields
and *yearn for her* becomes *Guernica*.

MODERNIST LOVE

Bored of the Modernists, he's trying
to hurry her to more erotic Movements.

She holds him back, entranced
by a vision of floating brides: the veils,
the trains, the faded bouquets. She mourns
the demise of everyone's marriages, guesses
romance dies in the kitchen, the laundry, et al.

He asks if she fancies a quick Chagall.

ROTHKO FOR DUMMIES

No connoisseur, I thought Portraits
and Landscapes were options
in my Printer Settings dialogue box,
but standing in this hush-light room,
I think I understand Rothko's swathes -
those slit-wrist-red meadows of pigment
stir something in me,
a recognition -
        Rothko painted in Broadband.

RESOLUTION

Seurat pointed the way-
he painted at 16 dots per inch,
presaging desktop bitmapped art,
increasing this couple's resolution
that they will never be
more than twenty pixels apart.

VINNOCENCE

Is it Van Goff, Van Gock or Van Go?
How do you say his name?

Do you cough it, do you choke it,
Does it set your throat aflame?

I simply call him Vincent,
like that song by Don McLean.

Vincent the innocent,
patron saint of paint and pain.

ANOTHER OLD PHOTOGRAPH POEM

I'm at the edge
of the frame, or just beyond the field
of vision: a glint, a reflection
in someone's glasses; a smudge
in the emulsion. I can nearly be seen
as a mote in my mother's eye, a gleam
in my father's. I'm almost anecdotal.
I could be behind that tree, a willow,
the wisp of a whisper, a fissure, a fracture
in time, a phantom, a spectre, but no, I forgot –
I'm taking the picture.

VENUS INFERS

Venus infers harmless love unsullied by all things worldly.
A planet devoted to sensuality and tactile topography,
nude photography and subtle analogy. She is anti pornography.

Venus mars no body. She is heavenly, heavy with yesses.
She blesses all with kisses, touches and caresses.
She comes out of her shell, all sweetness, breasts and tresses.

She's then introduced to musicians and politicians:
ends up in high-heels and masochists' imaginations-
kiss the whip, feel the rip of her sadistic machinations.

Shiny, shiny: all that glisters are your blisters.

DA CAPO

Every working hour's the same
as every hour that's passed away.
At home I sit and chant your name
and watch repeats of Groundhog Day.

HANNIBAL LECTERN

How silent the lambs
the poet chirped.

How silent the poet
the podium burped.

NOT ANOTHER BILLY COLLINS POEM

The room I write in at home is big enough for both
me and Billy Collins to go sailing around in.
So why is it that Billy can write a library of books
on rooms such as mine, with its view over the trees
of seven fields with nine horses, a mythological river
spanned by a metaphorical bridge that carries
consciousness from dream state to waking state,
a heron flying by, the tips of its wings seemingly
skimming the snow on the cap of that purple mountain
several Cairngorm miles in the distance, while I can only
write of such things in this dingy hotel on Princes Street,
a half-eaten burger in the bin, rain cascading down
the scaffolding outside the unopenable window, sirens
doppler shifting their way down to Broughton Street,
a faint smear of blood on the shower curtain, and that
unspeakable stain on the bedroom carpet that seems
to have crawled up the walls overnight?

STEREOTYPE

All I knew of him was his open face.
He lived his life in lower case. Others
knew the height of his caps, the only
x-heightment caused by the chap.

His character set his justified frown.
An old style bookman, words were his
wont. He lived in Lorem Ipsum town,
down by the foundry, down by the fount.

His life was a page with ragged edges,
his thoughts were Antique without
ascenders. His obit said he'd been out of
sorts. His failures had all been <u>underscored</u>

Marriage? A ligature of *doleful* and *yearn-*
his manhood proportioned that of a kern.
A child of the Univers, a man of his Times,
something gothic haunted his eyes.

Now he's sans hope, sans serif, sans breath:
the last full stop is the dot of Death.

The name in his hearse was florally rolled
in one thousand point Bereavement Bold.

JOHN MOTSON MEETS EMILY DICKINSON

Well, Emily, after last Saturday's performance you have
to admit that hope isn't the thing with feathers – a parrot is.

Hope is the Thing of Leather—
That Nestles in the Goal—
We Sing our Tunes, Belt out the Words—
You're Gonna win Fuck All—

The current crisis at Anfield is similar to the one you had
with Athletico Amherst last year, which you put down
to the team not touching the *This is Amherst* sign.
Can Liverpool turn their season around?

And sometimes—in a Gale—is Heard—
Walk On Through The Storm—
That Silver-songéd little Bird—
Kept the Faithful warm—

You're famous for your no-score-drawers. Have you ever
considered getting them off for the boys? Have those
atrocious refereeing decisions nearly defrosted you?

Not one of all the Purple Host—
Who took the Flag today—
Can tell the Definition—
So clear, of Victory—

You were very active in the technical area on Saturday.
It looked as though you were kicking every ball.
Have you ever considered picking yourself?

I've Shouted from the chilly Stand—
Sometimes at my TV—
At every Penalty, my Plea—
Please Hand the Ball – to Me—

Do you know what they say about you, Emily?

No, John, pray Tell—

They say you're always last in the showers.

Well, John, *someone* has to pick up the Soap—

THE PARADOX OF THE TWINS

He's twenty years my junior
although he is my brother,
although he is my twin.
He left this place two years ago for him.

He waved from his transporter.
We set our clocks in synchrony
to match our syncopated heartbeats.
It seemed the stars pulsed out their light
with an interstellar symphony
to greet his strange impending flight.

For me, dilated eyes; for him, dilated time.
The years between would test our relativity.

The last time I saw my face in his
he was smiling as he waved adieu.
It was so long ago.
It was so long ago.
 He was smiling as he waved adieu
the last time I saw my face in his.

The years between would test our relativity.
For me, dilated eyes, for him, dilated time.

To greet his strange impending flight
with an interstellar symphony
it seemed the stars pulsed out their light.
To match our syncopated heartbeats
we set our clocks in synchrony.
He waved from his transporter.

He left this place two years ago for him.
Although he is my twin,
although he is my brother,
he's twenty years my junior.

IN VIGIL, LATER

In junior school we took turns to be Milk Monitor, braving
brittle winter mornings to collect crates from the playground
and deliver frosted bottles of white ice to classmates.
Summer bottles held cocktails of curds, the stench
of which caused heaving seas of bile in twenty stomachs.
After seeing the nurse we became Pencil Monitors and
Ruler Monitors. Nowadays they have Computer Monitors.

This is recalled in the brimming dark of Ward 49,
the bleak pre-winter night outside fireflied with helicopters
full of offshore orderlies rushing to take the pulse of a Rig.
Crescendos of tiny sounds from bedside sentries beep
their way through corridor cacophonies; insistent signals
assessing the flow of fluids through ten thousand veins.

Beyond ward windows moonlight caresses lovers, pulls
back their blankets of darkness. Couples blushed and
flushed with sex glow in rude cocoons of health.

They are miles and years away from me but I sense them
out there, record their pulsing desires.

Tonight I am the Heart Monitor.

RUNNING OUT OF WORLD

The man in the bed next door
had a visit from his specialist.

Later that afternoon he got out of bed,
grabbed his stick and went for a short
breathless walk.

Isn't it great to get out of this room
and back in the world? I said.

*It won't be for long, I've just been told
I've got cancer.*

THE ONLY WAY OUT

He's had his biopsy results.

He leans over and tells me,
I'm on my way out.

You're going home?

No.

He makes the sign of the cross.

HARD TO SWALLOW

I've got bad news for you.
Here's the lunch menu...
The cancer is widespread.
Soup with croutons for starters
We've found lumps everywhere.
then meatballs
In your throat.
with sprouts
In your kidneys.
and peas
In your prostate.
or sweetcorn
You've got small-cell lung cancer.
with potatoes.
I'm afraid it's untreatable.
Treacle pudding
We'll make you as comfortable as possible.
with custard.
Sorry.
Or jelly?   Everyone loves the jelly.

IF YOU SEE A MAN

If you see a man weeping,
hold his hand.

If you see a man mourning,
hold his hand.

If you see a man mourning himself,
hold his hand.

If you see a man without hope,
hold his hand.

If you see a man asking for his family,
hold his hand.

If you see a man's wife holding his hand,
she will hold your hand in turn.

And you will be part of their family
until the curtains are drawn.

AT THE TOMB OF THE UNKNOWN ACCOUNTANT

Meet me tonight in the graveyard
where stars climb the graph of the sky,
when Orion skims over horizons
and the moon is a silver coin.

We'll kneel at the double-entry
to the tomb where the great man lies,
clutching the FTSE 100
in the fist of his cheque-signing hand.

Yes, he's clutching the FTSE 100
and a paperweight made out of gold.
His casket is made of old banknotes.
The handles are crocodile clips.

We'll visit his coffin at midnight,
spread sheets on the cold hard ground,
with prayers on our trembling lips
and dewy librarian eyes.

With dewy librarian eyes, my dear,
we'll read his great works out aloud:
his Hang Seng Opus, his Dow Jones Dirge,
his Ode to the Banks of the Nile.

He failed an internal audit
of his punctured Midas gland.
Gold dust got into his system
and poisoned his bullandbear heart.

He died, unknown to his clients,
in a far-flung foreign exchange.
He died, a loan in his wallet
from the Bonnie and Clydesdale bank.

At the tomb of the Unknown Accountant
wordsmiths wonder and awe,
who can't rub two pennies together,
whose book-keeping keeps them all poor.

Praise to the numerate masses
of this number-worshipping world.
Praise to their dexterous digits,
their Lottery Roll-Over souls.

Let us invoke all the Mammonite codes.
Let us recite the Lloyds Prayer.
Kneel with me here, for we are the meek
and we will inherit fuck all.

Though we will inherit fuck all, my love,
let us light this eternal flame.
For his is the power of eviction.
May the Lord repossess his soul.

To the tomb of the Unknown Accountant
we'll pilgrimage each fiscal Spring
on economy classes of transport
we'll make our annual returns.

A TERRACEFUL OF MARILYNS

This isn't Opera. No cosy fans will flutter,
unless it's a version of *The Flying Dutchman*
with Marco *Polo* Van Basten ghosting in
for a shipload of goals.

This isn't Ballet. No fouettés in Capezio canvas,
unless it's a score by Prokoviev, where Nureyev
dazzles: a blur of Cruyff turns from wing to wing.

This isn't a Broadway play. No dresser will deal
with scuffed shoes, unless *Cat on a Hot Tin Roof*
is proof Cantona ran hotfoot from Old Trafford.

This isn't Modern Art. No nancy boys will cry
for *MOMA*, unless the referee is blowing the whistle
of a train hurtling from the goalmouth, and a terraceful
of Marilyn Monroes are shouting: *this is not a pipe
dream!*

No-one wears a Tuxedo. None arrive at the turnstiles
in limousines zebra striped by neon lights.

People won't scream for encores and authors.
There will be no bows from the orchestra.
Only, here and there, twin strikers, seemingly asleep
in their boots, crouch like tigers in red leather.

WHY SHE FLEW TO BARCELONA

Why she flew to Barcelona
she wouldn't say, leaving
all to conjecture to this day.

Did somebody forsake her?
Never write and never phone her?
Did a panic overtake her?
Cause her manic departure?

Did she fly into a rage? Or fly
in the face of a Convention
guzzling duty-free Rioja
on its way to Zaragoza via
Palma de Mallorca or
the island of Ibiza?

Was it her Spanish roots, her title
Senorita? Was someone there to
meet her near *Sagrada Familia*?

Or was she flying there to meet
herself? Cast off the chains of
someone else and walk away, a loner
gambling on her future: no man
would have or own her on his terms
alone now she found herself *en casa?*

If you asked her now, she'd ask of you:
what could she do?

Why, she flew to Barcelona.

VOICE BOXING

My voice, my speech, are tanged with salt
air. My throat is coated with estuary winds
which whirled down Water Street to bluster
over the Goree Piazza, tripping the bronze-
sculpted buckets to tip their freight of Mersey
brine unspooling into sloop-shaped pools.

The dustings from the grist of mills accentuates
my accent: my coal-caked vocal chords vibrate
and resonate in the tonal range of tugs sluicing
silt from Ellesmere Port to Bromborough Dock.
All gutturals and glottal stops, all aitches dropped,
the lilt of which will warm or warn.

Know me by the sounds I utter – the guttersnipe
whine, scallywag snarl, knavish slaver, or sugar-
coated sibilants: clue in to the tremolo, tremor,
the whoop or whimper. Gather the gist from
an open hand, a closed fist, the pitch:
there, there; fuck you; I do.